Eye On The Environment

POISONED WATER

J.M. Patten, Ed.D.

The Rourke Book Co., Inc.
Vero Beach, Florida 32964

Edited by Pamela J.P. Schroeder and Sandra A. Robinson

PHOTO CREDITS
© J.M. Patten: cover, pages 4, 7, 9, 10, 12, 13, 15, 16, 18, 19, 21, 22; courtesy Janine Perky, U.S. Fish and Wildlife Service: page 6

Library of Congress Cataloging-in-Publication Data

Patten, J.M., 1944-
    Poisoned water / by J.M. Patten.
    p. cm. — (Eye on the environment)
    Includes index.
    ISBN 1-55916-097-7
    1. Water—Pollution—Juvenile literature.
[1. Water—Pollution. 2. Pollution.] I. Title. II. Series.
TD422.P38   1995
363.73'94—dc20   94-37163
                                             CIP
                                             AC

Printed in the USA

TABLE OF CONTENTS

EYE ON POISONED WATER

This book is about poisoned water. You will find out how clean water becomes **polluted,** or dirty water, that harms the Earth's **environment.**

The Earth's environment is all living and nonliving things in the world. The soil we farm, air we breathe, and water we drink are important parts of the environment. People must work to keep them clean and safe.

Earth is our home—the only known place where people, plants and animals can live. Poisoned water damages our home, hurting us all.

This sparkling New England river provides drinking water for thousands of people living in cities.

CLEAN WATER AND LIVING THINGS

Clean water is a **natural resource,** or something not made by people. Water covers three-fourths of the Earth.

People, plants and animals need clean water to live. A person can live about two months without food but only about seven days without water.

These pelicans will need help to survive after being trapped in spilled oil.

People need two quarts of clean water a day to stay healthy.

People need about two quarts of water a day to stay healthy. Some of this water comes from the milk and juice we drink, and the food we eat.

SALT WATER AND FRESH WATER

Most of the Earth's water is in the oceans. Ocean water contains salt and is called **salt water.** People cannot drink salt water. Too much salt water makes people—and many plants and animals—sick.

The rest of our water is **fresh water,** or water without lots of salt in it. We drink fresh water that comes from lakes, rivers and underground.

This pipe may empty polluted water into the ocean.

NOTICE

DO NOT SWIM
PLAY ON OR
AROUND PIPE

HOW WATER IS POLLUTED

People, plants and animals can't live without clean water. Yet, bad things are dumped into our water every day.

There are many laws against polluting water. However, some careless people pollute our water with garbage, wastes and poisons.

Today, many caring children and adults are worried about having enough clean water, both now and in the future.

Standing water in this ditch has been sprayed with a pesticide to kill mosquitoes. Is this water still safe for field animals and birds to drink?

POLLUTION FROM CITIES AND TOWNS

Many people live in cities and towns. They use huge amounts of water. In many communities, water is stored and cleaned after people have used it. This water can go into lakes, rivers and the ocean with no harm to the environment.

Waste from a nearby factory has turned this pond yellow with poison.

This sport fishing boat works against a strong current to get to open ocean.

In some cities and towns, **untreated** waste water from sinks, tubs and toilets pours right out of sewer pipes into rivers and lakes. This polluted water kills plants, animals and fish. It can even kill people.

POLLUTION FROM FARMS AND FACTORIES

Factories use tons and tons of water. Some of this water gets very dirty and goes right into our **water supply**—the water we use.

Farms use **fertilizer,** or plant food, to help plants grow. Rain can wash fertilizer into lakes and rivers. This harms the environment.

Sometimes pollution is natural. Rain washes body waste from herds of farm animals into the water.

Untreated water from cities and factories is a major environmental problem for rivers and lakes.

POLLUTION OF THE OCEANS

Some scientists say pollution is killing our great oceans. Today, trash and oil float on ocean water almost everywhere.

In some places, garbage boats go to sea at night to dump trash and waste. Ships spill oil on ocean water almost every day. Dirty rivers empty pollution from farms and factories into the ocean.

We once thought that the oceans were so big we could dump anything we wanted into them. Today, we know we are hurting our ocean environment—and hurting ourselves.

This fast growth of algae was probably caused by plant fertilizer that washed into this lake during a rainstorm.

CLEAN WATER FOR PLAYING

Clean water isn't just for drinking or taking a bath. Water is fun to play in, too.

We need to keep our water clean and safe for playing and relaxing.

These young surfers are eager to catch a wave.

Clean water makes the fishing good, and many people come to catch dinner.

Some people love to swim and canoe. Others sail and water-ski. People fish, crab and clam for fun and food. Do you go ice skating?

SAVING OUR WATER

Each and every one of us can help to fight pollution and keep our water clean. Here are some ways you can help.

Use only the water you need. Take shorter showers. Use less in the tub. Turn off the water when you brush your teeth.

Keep our water supply clean. Put trash in its proper place—not in the water.

If you spot a pollution problem, tell people about it. When your town has a river, lake or beach cleanup day, go and help make the water sparkle.

In many places, treated or cleaned water is used to water parks, lawns and golf courses.

GLOSSARY

environment (en VI ren ment) — the world around us including plants, animals, soil, water and air

fertilizer (FUR tuh li zer) — plant food

fresh water (FRESH WAH ter) — water without salt; found in most lakes and rivers

natural resource (NA chur uhl REE sors) — useful things that are not made by people

polluted (puh LOOT ed) — too dirty to use

salt water (SALT WAH ter) — water with lots of salt in it; mostly ocean and sea water

untreated (un TREET ed) — polluted water from farms, factories and sewers that people have not tried to clean

water supply (WAH ter suh PLY) — the clean water we need and use

Clean, fresh spring water fills this old-fashioned wooden tub at a country camp.

INDEX